# Christmas Cookies

## Delicious treats for the festive season

igloobooks

igloobooks

Published in 2015
by Igloo Books Ltd
Cottage Farm
Sywell
NN6 0BJ
www.igloobooks.com


The measurements used are approximate.



FIR003 0815
2 4 6 8 10 9 7 5 3
ISBN 978-1-78440-975-3

Printed and manufactured in China

# Contents

# Christmas Classics

# Iced Gingerbread

**Makes** 24 **Preparation time** 2 hours 25–30 minutes **Cooking time** 10–12 minutes

## Ingredients

300 g / 10 ½ oz / 2 cups plain (all-purpose) flour, sifted

a little extra plain flour, for dusting

1 tsp baking powder

½ tsp bicarbonate of (baking) soda

a pinch of salt

2 tsp ground ginger

110 g / 4 oz / ½ cup unsalted butter, softened

110 g / 4 oz / ⅔ cup soft dark brown sugar

75 g / 3 oz / ¼ cup treacle

1 tsp vanilla extract

1 small egg, lightly beaten

a small handful of seedless red grapes

2 tbsp powdered gelatin

75 g / 3 oz / ⅓ cup caster (superfine) sugar

white icing pen

## Method

1. Combine the flour, baking powder, bicarbonate of soda, salt and ginger in a large mixing bowl, stirring thoroughly.
2. Beat together the butter, brown sugar, treacle and vanilla extract in a separate bowl until thick. Stir in the beaten egg until incorporated.
3. Gradually add the dry ingredients to the bowl, mixing well, until a dough comes together. Gather the dough and wrap loosely in a sheet of greaseproof paper.
4. Leave the dough to stand at room temperature for 2 hours.
5. Rinse the grapes in a colander and combine the gelatin and sugar in a mixing bowl, then add the grapes to the bowl and stir well to coat in the sugar mixture.
6. Arrange them on a lined tray and chill for 1 hour.
7. Preheat the oven to 190°C (170°C fan) / 375F / gas 5 and line two baking trays with greaseproof paper.
8. Dust a work surface with flour and roll out the dough on it to 5 mm (¼ in) thickness.
9. Use a square cookie cutter to stamp out squares of dough, arranging them on the trays, spaced apart.
10. Bake for 10–12 minutes until golden and set.
11. Remove from the oven and leave to rest on the trays for 5 minutes, then move to a wire rack to finish cooling.
12. Once cool, decorate the squares using the icing pen, icing them with ribbon and bows.
13. Serve with the frosted grapes on the side.

# Vanilla Moons

**Makes** 16 **Preparation time** 25–30 minutes **Cooking time** 12–16 minutes

## Ingredients

300 g / 10 ½ oz / 1 ⅓ cups margarine, softened

225 g / 8 oz / 1 cup caster (superfine) sugar

400 g / 14 oz / 2 ⅔ cups plain (all-purpose) flour, sifted

a little extra plain flour, for dusting

1 tsp bicarbonate of (baking) soda

1 tsp vanilla extract

a pinch of salt

250 g / 9 oz / 2 cups icing (confectioners') sugar, sifted

2–3 tbsp boiling water

a pinch of ground cloves

a few threads of saffron, chopped

a small sheet of edible gold leaf

## Method

1. Preheat the oven to 160°C (140°C fan) / 325F / gas 3 and grease and line two baking trays with greaseproof paper.
2. Cream the margarine and sugar in a mixing bowl until fluffy and pale.
3. Beat in the flour, bicarbonate of soda, vanilla extract and salt, then knead gently for 2–3 minutes.
4. Roll out to 5 mm thickness on a floured surface and use a half-moon shaped fluted cutter to stamp out 32 dough shapes.
5. Arrange on the baking trays, spaced apart and bake for 12–16 minutes until set.
6. Remove the cookies from the oven and leave them to cool on their trays for a few minutes.
7. Move the cookies to a wire rack to finish cooling.
8. Whisk the icing sugar with enough boiling water until smooth and of spreadable consistency.
9. Add the ground cloves and the chopped saffron and mix briefly to incorporate.
10. Spread the cookies with a thin layer of the icing using a small palette knife.
11. Stack the cookies in pairs to sandwich together.
12. Garnish with a little gold leaf, using a pair of kitchen tweezers to separate and place on the cookies before serving.

# Christmas Pudding Bites

**Makes** 24 **Preparation time** 1 hour 20–25 minutes **Cooking time** 12–15 minutes

## Ingredients

55 g / 2 oz / ⅓ cup raisins
2 tbsp currants
2 tbsp chopped mixed peel
2 tbsp brandy
100 g / 3 ½ oz / ½ cup unsalted butter, softened
65 g / 2 ½ oz / ⅓ cup light brown sugar
1 tbsp finely grated orange zest
1 tbsp treacle, warmed
1 tsp ground allspice
2 tbsp flaked (slivered) almonds
200 g / 7 oz / 1 ⅓ cups self-raising flour, sifted
2 tbsp ground almonds
200 g / 7 oz / 1 cup demerara sugar
200 g / 7 oz / 2 cups white royal icing sugar
1 tbsp lemon juice
a small handful of glacé cherries, cut into small pieces
a few mint leaves

## Method

1. Combine the dried fruit with the brandy in a mixing bowl. Stir and leave to sit for 1 hour.
2. Tip into a food processor and blend until fairly smooth.
3. Preheat the oven to 190°C (170°C fan) / 375F / gas 5 and line two baking trays with greaseproof paper.
4. Beat together the butter, sugar and zest.
5. Add the treacle to the butter mixture, along with the spice, mixing well.
6. Add the flaked almonds, flour, ground almonds and fruit mixture from the processor.
7. Roll the mixture into walnut-sized balls with your hands and then roll each ball in the demerara sugar and place on the baking trays, spaced apart.
8. Bake for 12–15 minutes until the biscuits look dry and slightly cracked on the surface. Cool on the trays for 5 minutes, then place on a wire rack to cool completely.
9. Beat together the royal icing and lemon juice in a bowl until thick and smooth, adding a little hot water to thin it out if necessary.
10. Spoon a little icing onto each cake, allowing it to run down the sides, to resemble snow.
11. Add a piece of cherry and a mint leaf to each cake and leave to set before serving.

# Chocolate Florentines

**Makes** 18 **Preparation time** 40–45 minutes **Cooking time** 10–15 minutes

## Ingredients

110 g / 4 oz / ½ cup unsalted butter

75 g / 3 oz / ¼ cup golden syrup

75 g / 3 oz / ¾ cup walnut halves, roughly chopped

75 g / 3 oz / ¾ cup flaked (slivered) almonds

300 g / 10 ½ oz / 2 cups dried tropical fruit mix

450 g / 1 lb / 3 cups good-quality dark chocolate, chopped

1 tbsp liquid glucose

## Method

1. Melt together the butter and golden syrup in a saucepan set over a medium heat.
2. Once melted, add the walnut halves, flaked almonds and dried tropical fruit, stirring thoroughly until combined.
3. Line a large baking tray with greaseproof paper.
4. Place the chopped chocolate and glucose in a heatproof bowl set over a half-filled saucepan of gently simmering water.
5. Stir occasionally until melted, then remove from the heat.
6. Spoon rounds of melted chocolate onto the greaseproof paper and leave them to set for 1 minute.
7. Spoon the fruit and nut mixture on top of the rounds of setting chocolate.
8. Chill for 20 minutes until set, then remove from the fridge and peel away from the greaseproof paper before serving in paper cases.

# Iced Star Cookies

**Makes** 24 **Preparation time** 1 hour 35 minutes **Cooking time** 15–18 minutes

## Ingredients

300 g / 10 ½ oz / 2 cups plain (all-purpose) flour

a little extra plain flour, for dusting

225 g / 8 oz / 1 cup unsalted butter, melted and cooled

165 g / 5 ½ oz / 1 ⅓ cups icing (confectioners') sugar

a little extra icing sugar, for dusting

50 g / 2 oz / ⅓ cup cornflour (cornstarch)

55 g / 2 oz / ¼ cup caster (superfine) sugar

450 g / 1 lb / 2 cups white fondant icing

75 g / 3 oz / ⅓ cup apricot jam, warmed

150 g / 5 oz / 1 cup 'hundreds and thousands'

## Method

1. Mix together the flour, butter, icing sugar and cornflour in a mixing bowl until it comes together as a dough.
2. Knead briefly, then wrap and chill for 1 hour.
3. Preheat the oven to 180°C (160°C fan) / 350F / gas 4 and line two baking trays with greaseproof paper.
4. Roll out the dough on a floured surface to 1 cm (½ in) thickness and cut out 24 stars using a star-shaped cookie cutter.
5. Arrange the stars on the trays, spaced apart, and bake for 15–18 minutes until golden-brown in appearance.
6. Remove the cookies to a wire rack to cool.
7. Roll out the fondant icing to 1 cm (½ in) thickness on a clean surface dusted with a little icing sugar.
8. Using two similarly proportioned star-shaped cutters, stamp out icing stars, creating some shapes using two at the same time to make thin borders of icing for the cookies.
9. Brush the tops of the cooled cookies with a little apricot jam, then decorate with the fondant icing shapes.
10. Fill in the borders using hundreds and thousands before serving.

# Mini Stollen

**Makes** 16 **Preparation time** 1 hour 40–45 minutes **Cooking time** 25–30 minutes

## Ingredients

125 ml / 4 ½ fl. oz / ½ cup whole milk, warmed
2 tsp dried active yeast
250 g / 9 oz / 1 ⅔ cups plain (all-purpose) flour, sifted
a little extra plain flour, for dusting
a pinch of salt
1 tsp ground mixed spice
1 tsp ground cinnamon
1 tbsp caster (superfine) sugar
65 g / 2 ½ oz / ¼ cup unsalted butter, softened
1 large egg, lightly beaten
55 g / 2 oz / ½ cup ground almonds
150 g / 5 oz / 1 cup mixed candied peel, chopped
150 g / 5 oz / 1 cup sultanas
125 g / 4 ½ oz / 1 cup icing (confectioners') sugar, for dusting

## Method

1. Combine the warmed milk and yeast in a mixing bowl and leave for 5 minutes.
2. Mix together the flour, salt, ground spices and sugar in a large mixing bowl, then add the butter, egg, ground almonds, mixed candied peel and sultanas and mix well.
3. Add the milk and yeast mixture to the bowl and stir well until it comes together as a dough.
4. Turn out onto a lightly floured surface and knead for 5–6 minutes until even and smooth, then cover with a damp tea towel and leave to prove for 20 minutes.
5. After proving, knock the dough back and knead again for a further 5 minutes.
6. Divide the dough into 16 equal pieces and shape into small rounds, placing them on a greased baking tray.
7. Cover with a damp tea towel and leave them to prove in a warm place for 1 hour.
8. Preheat the oven to 180°C (160°C fan) / 350F / gas 4.
9. Bake the stollen for 25–30 minutes until risen and golden on the outside, then remove from the oven and transfer to a wire rack to cool.
10. Roll the mini stollen in the icing sugar as they cool, serving them warm or once cooled.

# Christmas Biscotti

**Makes** 48 **Preparation time** 1 hour 10 minutes **Cooking time** 35–45 minutes

## Ingredients

- 350 g / 12 oz / 2 ⅓ cups plain (all-purpose) flour
- 1 tsp baking powder
- ¼ tsp bicarbonate of (baking) soda
- a pinch of salt
- 2 medium eggs
- 125 ml / 4 ½ fl. oz / ½ cup sunflower oil
- 225 g / 8 oz / 1 cup honey
- 75 g / 3 oz / ⅓ cup caster (superfine) sugar
- 1 tsp vanilla extract
- 1 orange, zested
- 175 g / 6 oz / 1 ½ cups almonds, toasted and chopped
- 175 g / 6 oz / 1 ¼ cups pitted dates, chopped
- 1 medium egg white

## Method

1. Mix the flour with the baking powder, bicarbonate of soda and a pinch of salt in a large mixing bowl.
2. In a separate bowl, whisk together the eggs, oil, honey, sugar, vanilla extract and orange zest, then add the flour mixture and stir well to incorporate.
3. Knead in the almonds and dates, then cover and chill for 30 minutes.
4. Preheat the oven to 190°C (170°C fan) / 375F / gas 5 and line a large baking tray with greaseproof paper.
5. Divide the dough in two and then shape each piece into a sausage shape roughly 40 cm (16 in) long and 5 cm (2 in) wide.
6. Place on the baking tray, leaving a gap between each piece.
7. Lightly beat the egg white with a splash of water and brush over the dough.
8. Bake for 20–25 minutes until golden on top and just starting to crack.
9. Remove from the oven and leave to cool on the trays for 15 minutes.
10. Reduce the oven to 150°C (130°C fan) / 300F / gas 2.
11. Cut each sausage of dough into roughly 1 cm (½ in) slices and return to the baking tray on their ends.
12. Bake for a further 15–20 minutes until golden at the edges and dry at the centre.
13. Remove from the oven and leave to cool on wire racks before serving.

# Panforte Slices

**Makes** 24 **Preparation time** 20 minutes **Cooking time** 1 hour 5–10 minutes

## Ingredients

225 g / 8 oz / 1 cup dried prunes, soaked in hot water

150 g / 5 oz / 1 cup raisins, soaked in hot water

2 tbsp cocoa powder

100 g / 3 ½ oz / ⅔ cup plain (all-purpose) flour

½ tsp ground cinnamon

½ tsp ground ginger

¼ tsp salt

110 g / 4 oz / 1 cup blanched almonds

110 g / 4 oz / 1 cup blanched hazelnuts (cobnuts)

175 g / 6 oz / 1 cup soft light brown sugar

110 g / 4 oz / ½ cup honey

## Method

1. Preheat the oven to 150°C (130°C fan) / 300F / gas 2 and grease and line an 18 cm (7 in) square tin with greaseproof paper.
2. Blitz the prunes and raisins in a food processor with some of their soaking liquid until smooth. Set to one side.
3. Combine the cocoa powder, flour, spices, salt and nuts in a large mixing bowl.
4. Stir together the sugar and honey in a saucepan. Cook over a medium heat until the sugar has dissolved and you have a golden syrup. Increase the heat and boil, without stirring, until the mixture registers 116°C / 240F on a sugar thermometer.
5. Pour the syrup over the flour and nuts and mix quickly and thoroughly until combined. Add the puréed prunes and raisins and stir well.
6. Working quickly, scrape into the prepared tin and use damp hands to flatten the top evenly. Bake for 45–55 minutes until the edges start to rise slightly and appear matte.
7. Remove to a wire rack to cool. Turn out once cool and cut into slices before serving.

# Iced Snowmen with Eggnog

**Serves** 4 **Preparation time** 4 hours 35–40 minutes **Cooking time** 15–18 minutes

## Ingredients

**For the cookies:**

110 g / 4 oz / ½ cup unsalted butter, softened

85 g / 3 oz / ⅓ cup caster (superfine) sugar

1 small egg, lightly beaten

1 ½ tsp vanilla extract

150 g / 5 oz / 1 cup plain (all-purpose) flour, sifted

a little extra plain flour, for dusting

1 tbsp cornflour (cornstarch)

a pinch of salt

white icing pen

**For the eggnog:**

4 medium egg yolks

90 g / 3 oz / ⅓ cup caster (superfine) sugar

600 ml / 1 pint 2 fl. oz / 2 ½ cups whole milk

250 ml / 9 fl. oz / 1 cup double (heavy) cream

2 tsp freshly grated nutmeg

100 ml / 3 ½ fl. oz / ½ cup bourbon

a few cinnamon sticks, to garnish

## Method

1. For the cookies: beat together the butter and sugar in a large mixing bowl until pale and fluffy.
2. Add the beaten egg and half the vanilla, mixing well.
3. Add the flour, cornflour and salt and mix until a dough comes together. Wrap the dough in cling film and chill for 1 hour.
4. Preheat the oven to 180°C (160°C fan) / 350F / gas 4 and line two large baking trays with greaseproof paper.
5. On a lightly floured surface, roll out the dough to 5 mm thickness.
6. Using a snowman cookie cutter, cut out snowmen from the dough and arrange on the baking trays, well spaced apart. Bake for 15–18 minutes until golden and set, then remove from the oven.
7. Leave the cookies to cool on their trays for a few minutes before moving to wire racks to finish cooling.
8. Once cool, decorate the snowmen with an icing pen, leaving them to set.
9. For the eggnog: beat together the egg yolks and sugar in a heatproof mixing bowl until pale and thick.
10. Combine the milk, cream and nutmeg in a saucepan set over a medium heat and warm until the mixture starts to boil.
11. Remove from the heat and gradually whisk into the egg yolks and sugar mixture.
12. Strain the mixture back into a clean saucepan and cook over a medium heat, stirring constantly, until it registers 72°C / 162F on a sugar thermometer.
13. Stir through the bourbon and let the mixture cool slightly.
14. Pour the eggnog into a clean bowl and cover and chill for 3 hours until cold, then ladle into glasses and garnish with cinnamon sticks, serving with the biscuits.

# Indulgent

# Double Chocolate Cookies

**Makes** 18 **Preparation time** 15 minutes **Cooking time** 15 minutes

## Ingredients

175 g / 6 oz / 1 ¼ cups plain (all-purpose) flour

55 g / 2 oz / ⅓ cup cocoa powder

½ tsp salt

½ tsp bicarbonate of (baking) soda

110 g / 4 oz / ½ cup unsalted butter, softened

175 g / 6 oz / 1 cup soft light brown sugar

1 large egg, beaten

½ tsp vanilla extract

2 tbsp whole milk

100 g / 3 ½ oz / ⅔ cup dark chocolate chips

## Method

1. Preheat the oven to 180°C (160°C fan) / 350F / gas 4 and line two large baking trays with greaseproof paper.
2. Sift together the flour, cocoa powder, salt and bicarbonate of soda in a large mixing bowl.
3. Cream together the butter, sugar, egg and vanilla extract in a separate mixing bowl until pale and fluffy.
4. Fold the dry ingredients into the creamed butter mixture until a cookie dough comes together, then stir in the milk and chocolate chips.
5. Drop small balls of the dough onto the baking trays, spaced apart, and flatten them slightly with the back of a tablespoon.
6. Bake for 10–12 minutes until firm and set. Remove to a wire rack to cool before serving.

# Brandy Snaps

**Makes** 24 **Preparation time** 15 minutes **Cooking time** 20 minutes

## Ingredients

2 tbsp sunflower oil

110 g / 4 oz / ½ cup butter, softened

110 g / 4 oz / ⅔ cup soft light brown sugar

100 g / 3 ½ oz / ⅓ cup golden syrup

1 tbsp brandy

100 g / 3 ½ oz / ⅔ cup plain (all-purpose) flour

¼ tsp ground ginger

55 g / 2 oz / ½ cup flaked (slivered) almonds

## Method

1. Preheat the oven to 180°C (160°C fan) / 350F / gas 4 and line two large baking trays with greaseproof paper. Grease the tops of the paper with the sunflower oil.
2. Melt together the butter, sugar, golden syrup and brandy in a saucepan set over a medium heat. Stir occasionally until smooth.
3. Combine the flour and ground ginger in a large mixing bowl, making a well in the centre. Pour the melted butter mixture into the well and start to incorporate into the flour until thoroughly combined.
4. Drop generous teaspoons of the mixture onto the lined baking trays, spacing them apart and spreading out into rounds. Top half with flaked almonds.
5. Bake for 8–10 minutes until dark golden and set. Remove from the oven and leave to cool for 1 minute, then curl some over a rolling pin and roll others around a sharpening steel to create different shapes.
6. Leave them to cool and set before serving.

# Peanut Butter Cookies

**Makes** 24 **Preparation time** 15 minutes **Cooking time** 16–18 minutes

## Ingredients

225 g / 8 oz / 1 cup unsalted butter, softened
175 g / 6 oz / ¾ cup smooth peanut butter
175 g / 6 oz / 1 cup soft light brown sugar
1 large egg
½ tsp vanilla extract
150 g / 5 oz / 1 cup plain (all-purpose) flour
¾ tsp bicarbonate of (baking) soda
100 g / 3 ½ oz / ⅔ cup dark chocolate chips
110 g / 4 oz / 1 cup peanuts

## Method

1. Preheat the oven to 180°C (160°C fan) / 350F / gas 4 and line two large baking trays with greaseproof paper.
2. Cream together the butter, peanut butter and sugar in a large mixing bowl for 2–3 minutes until pale and smooth.
3. Add the egg and vanilla and mix again until incorporated. Fold through the flour and bicarbonate of soda until the dough comes together, then fold through the chocolate chips.
4. Drop tablespoons of the dough onto the lined baking trays, flattening them slightly with the back of the spoon. Stud with peanuts and bake for 16–18 minutes until golden at the edges and set.
5. Remove to a wire rack to cool before serving.

# White Chocolate Cookies

**Makes** 24 **Preparation time** 45 minutes **Cooking time** 25 minutes

## Ingredients

150 g / 5 oz / 1 cup white chocolate, chopped

350 g / 12 oz / 1 ½ cups unsalted butter, softened

55 g / 2 oz / ½ cup ground almonds

1 ½ tsp vanilla extract

55 g / 2 oz / ½ cup ground hazelnuts (cobnuts)

175 g / 6 oz / ¾ cup granulated sugar

¼ tsp salt

1 large egg yolk

300 g / 10 ½ oz / 2 cups plain (all-purpose) flour, sifted

2 tbsp icing (confectioners') sugar

## Method

1. Melt together the chocolate and 125 g / 4 oz / ½ cup of the butter in a heatproof bowl set atop a half-filled saucepan of simmering water. Stir occasionally until smooth, then remove from the heat.
2. Divide between two bowls. Add the ground almonds and ½ tsp of vanilla extract to one and the ground hazelnuts to the other, stirring well. Cover and leave to cool to one side.
3. In a large mixing bowl, cream together the remaining butter with the granulated sugar, salt and remaining vanilla extract until pale and fluffy.
4. Add the egg yolk and beat well, then fold in the flour until a dough comes together. Turn it out from the bowl and knead gently until even. Wrap in cling film and chill for 30 minutes.
5. Preheat the oven to 170°C (150°C fan) / 325F / gas 3 and line two large baking trays with greaseproof paper.
6. Remove the dough from the fridge and roll into a long cylinder, approximately 5 cm (2 in) in diameter. Use a sharp knife to cut into 2.5 mm (¼ in) rounds, spacing them apart on the baking trays.
7. Cut out small star shapes from half the rounds using a cutter or freehand using the tip of a sharp knife.
8. Bake for 16–18 minutes until set and starting to brown at the edges. Remove to a wire rack to cool.
9. Spread the complete round cookies with the white chocolate filling, sandwiching them against the star cookies. Dust with icing sugar before serving.

# Marzipan Cookies

**Makes** 24 **Preparation time** 1 hour 20 minutes **Cooking time** 12–14 minutes

## Ingredients

225 g / 8 oz / 1 cup marzipan, broken into small pieces

100 g / 3 ½ oz / ¾ cup icing (confectioners') sugar, plus extra for dusting

75 g / 3 oz / ¾ cup ground almonds

55 g / 2 oz / ⅓ cup plain (all-purpose) flour, plus extra for dusting

1 tsp rose water

1 medium egg white

75 g / 3 oz / ¾ cup flaked (slivered) almonds, chopped

## Method

1. Combine the marzipan pieces with the icing sugar, ground almonds, flour, rose water and egg white in a large mixing bowl. Mix with your hands until an even dough comes together.
2. Wrap the dough in cling film and chill for 1 hour.
3. Preheat the oven to 170°C (150°C fan) / 325F / gas 3 and line two large baking trays with greaseproof paper.
4. Remove the cookie dough from the fridge and shape generous teaspoons into rounds using floured hands. Space them apart on the baking trays and stud gently with the chopped almonds.
5. Bake for 12–14 minutes until golden brown at the edges and set. Remove to a wire rack to cool, dusting with icing sugar before serving.

# Chocolate Caramel Cookies

**Makes** 18 **Preparation time** 15 minutes **Cooking time** 8–10 minutes

## Ingredients

150 g / 5 oz / ⅔ cup unsalted butter, softened

225 g / 8 oz / 1 ⅓ cups soft light brown sugar

1 large egg

1 tsp vanilla extract

150 g / 5 oz / 1 cup plain (all-purpose) flour

55 g / 2 oz / ⅓ cup cocoa powder

½ tsp bicarbonate of (baking) soda

¼ tsp salt

2 chocolate, caramel and nougat bars, chopped

½ tsp flaked sea salt

## Method

1. Preheat the oven to 180°C (160°C fan) / 350F / gas 4 and line two large baking trays with greaseproof paper.
2. Cream together the butter and sugar in a large mixing bowl for 2–3 minutes until pale and fluffy.
3. Add the egg and vanilla extract, beating well until incorporated. Fold through the flour, cocoa powder, bicarbonate of soda and salt until a dough comes together.
4. Stir in the chopped caramel nougat bars and drop generous tablespoons of the dough onto the baking trays, spaced apart.
5. Bake for 8–10 minutes until just set. Remove to a wire rack and leave to cool slightly. Serve with a garnish of flaked sea salt on top.

# Almond Cookies with Hot Cocoa

**Makes** 24 (cookies) **Preparation time** 45 minutes **Cooking time** 30 minutes

## Ingredients

**For the cookies:**

110 g / 4 oz / ½ cup unsalted butter, softened

100 g / 3 ½ oz / ½ cup granulated sugar

¼ tsp salt

1 tsp vanilla extract

1 small egg yolk

150 g / 5 oz / 1 cup plain (all-purpose) flour, sifted

150 g / 5 oz / 1 cup white chocolate, chopped

1 tsp liquid glucose

55 g / 2 oz / ½ cup flaked (slivered) almonds, roughly chopped

**For the cocoa:**

900 ml / 1 pint 12 fl. oz / 3 ½ cups whole milk

150 ml / 5 fl. oz / ⅔ cup double (heavy) cream

55 g / 2 oz / ⅓ cup cocoa powder

125 g / 4 ½ oz / ½ cup caster (superfine) sugar

½ tsp vanilla extract

4 peppermint candy canes

## Method

1. For the cookies: in a large mixing bowl, cream together the butter, granulated sugar, salt and vanilla extract until pale and fluffy.
2. Add the egg yolk and beat well, then fold through the flour until a dough comes together. Turn out the dough from the bowl and knead gently to bring it together. Wrap in cling film and chill for 30 minutes.
3. Preheat the oven to 170°C (150°C fan) / 325F / gas 3 and line two large baking trays with greaseproof paper.
4. Remove the dough from the fridge and roll into a long cylinder, approximately 5 cm (2 in) in diameter. Use a sharp knife to cut into 2.5 mm (¼ in) rounds, spacing them apart on the baking trays. Cut out small holes from the rounds using the tip of a sharp knife.
5. Bake for 12–14 minutes until set and starting to brown at the edges. Remove to a wire rack to cool.
6. Melt together the chocolate and liquid glucose in a heatproof bowl set atop a half-filled saucepan of simmering water. Stir occasionally until smooth and then remove from the heat.
7. Spoon the mixture over the cooling cookies and sprinkle with chopped almonds, leaving the chocolate to set.
8. For the cocoa: warm together the milk and cream in a saucepan set over a medium heat. Stir together the cocoa powder and sugar in a heatproof bowl.
9. Whisk a little of the hot milk and cream mixture into the cocoa and sugar until you have a smooth paste. Stir in the remaining milk mixture, then return everything to the saucepan.
10. Simmer for 2 minutes, stirring in the remaining vanilla extract. Pour into mugs and garnish with candy canes and serve with the cookies on the side.

# Spiced

# Snickerdoodles and Poppy Seed Cookies

**Makes** 24 **Preparation time** 1 hour 20–25 minutes **Cooking time** 12–15 minutes

## Ingredients

450 g / 1 lb / 3 cups plain (all-purpose) flour
1 ½ tsp baking powder
1 tsp bicarbonate of (baking) soda
½ tsp salt
225 g / 8 oz / 1 cup unsalted butter, softened
225 g / 8 oz / 1 cup caster (superfine) sugar
2 large eggs, lightly beaten
2 tsp vanilla extract
1 tsp ground cinnamon, plus extra for sprinkling
100 g / 3 ½ oz / ¾ cup black poppy seeds
75 g / 3 oz / ⅓ cup granulated sugar

## Method

1. Combine the flour, baking powder, bicarbonate of soda and salt in a large mixing bowl, stirring thoroughly.
2. Cream together the butter and sugar in a separate mixing bowl for 3–4 minutes until pale and fluffy, then add the eggs and vanilla extract, beating again thoroughly to incorporate.
3. Mix in the dry ingredients in three additions, then divide the mixture between two bowls.
4. Add the ground cinnamon to one dough, mixing well.
5. Add the poppy seeds to the other, mixing until well incorporated into the dough.
6. Shape each dough into a cylinder and wrap in cling film, chilling for 1 hour.
7. Preheat the oven to 180°C (160°C fan) / 350F / gas 4 and line two large baking trays with greaseproof paper.
8. Remove the cookie dough from the fridge and slice into 1 cm (½ in) cookies using a sharp knife.
9. Arrange on the baking trays, spaced apart, and top with a little granulated sugar.
10. Bake for 12–15 minutes until golden on top and set, then remove from the oven and leave the cookies to cool on their trays for 5 minutes.
11. Move the cookies to a wire rack to finish cooling, garnishing with a sprinkle of ground cinnamon before serving.

# Cinnamon and Raisin Stars

**Makes** 24 **Preparation time** 30 minutes **Cooking time** 12–14 minutes

## Ingredients

225 g / 8 oz / 1 cup caster (superfine) sugar

125 g / 4 ½ oz / ½ cup unsalted butter, softened

1 large egg, lightly beaten

1 tsp vanilla extract

225 g / 8 oz / 1 ½ cups plain (all-purpose) flour, sifted

a little extra plain flour, for dusting

1 tsp baking powder

1 ½ tsp ground cinnamon, plus extra for dusting

a pinch of salt

100 g / 3 ½ oz / ⅔ cup raisins

a little icing (confectioners') sugar, for dusting

## Method

1. Preheat the oven to 180°C (160°C fan) / 350F / gas 4 and line a large baking tray with greaseproof paper.
2. Cream together the sugar and butter in a large mixing bowl for 3–4 minutes until pale and fluffy.
3. Add the egg and vanilla extract, beating well for a further minute, then add the flour, baking powder, cinnamon and salt, mixing well into a dough.
4. Add the raisins and mix until well incorporated.
5. Turn out the dough and knead briefly and gently into a ball, then roll out the dough on a lightly floured surface to 1 cm (½ in) thickness.
6. Using a star-shaped cutter, stamp out stars of dough and arrange on the baking tray, spaced apart.
7. Bake for 12–14 minutes until golden and set, then remove from the oven and leave the biscuits to cool on the trays for 10 minutes.
8. Mix the icing sugar with a little more ground cinnamon and dust over the cookies as they cool.
9. Serve once cool.

# Aniseed Cookies

**Makes** 18 **Preparation time** 1 hour 20 minutes + resting overnight **Cooking time** 30–35 minutes

## Ingredients

2 medium eggs

225 g / 8 oz / 2 cups icing (confectioners') sugar, sifted

2 tsp grated lemon zest

2 tsp ground aniseed

250 g / 9 oz / 1 ⅔ cups plain (all-purpose) flour, plus extra for dusting

¾ tsp baking powder

2 medium eggs

a few drops of anise extract

110 g / 4 oz / ½ cup caster (superfine) sugar

## Method

1. Whisk the eggs and icing sugar in a large mixing bowl until thick and light.
2. Stir in the lemon zest and ground aniseed until well incorporated, then sift in the flour and baking powder and mix well to form a dough.
3. Wrap in cling film and chill for 1 hour.
4. Line two large baking trays with greaseproof paper.
5. Roll out the dough on a lightly floured surface, to 1 cm (½ in) thickness.
6. Cut into small rounds and place on the baking trays and leave to stand uncovered, overnight.
7. Preheat the oven to 170°C (150°C fan) / 325F / gas 3.
8. Beat the egg whites with a pinch of salt in a large, clean mixing bowl until stiffly peaked. Beat in the anise extract and then the caster sugar, 1 tbsp at a time, until the meringue is thick and glossy.
9. Spoon into a piping bag fitted with a wide, round nozzle and pipe on top of the dried rounds.
10. Bake for 30–35 minutes until cooked and firm but still pale on top.
11. Cool on the baking trays for a few minutes,then move to a wire rack to finish cooling.
12. Serve once cool.

# Almond Gingerbread

**Makes** 24 **Preparation time** 2 hours 25–30 minutes **Cooking time** 12–14 minutes

## Ingredients

250 g / 9 oz / 1 ⅔ cups plain (all-purpose) flour, sifted
a little extra plain flour, for dusting
55 g / 2 oz / ½ cup ground almonds
1 tsp baking powder
½ tsp bicarbonate of (baking) soda
a pinch of salt
2 tsp ground ginger
1 tsp ground cloves
110 g / 4 oz / ½ cup unsalted butter, softened
110 g / 4 oz / ⅔ cup soft dark brown sugar
75 g / 3 oz / ¼ cup treacle
1 tsp vanilla extract
1 small egg, lightly beaten
150 g / 5 oz / 1 ½ cups blanched almonds
a large handful of glacé cherries

## Method

1. Stir together the flour, ground almonds, baking powder, bicarbonate of soda, salt, ginger and ground cloves in a mixing bowl.
2. Beat together the butter, soft dark brown sugar, treacle and vanilla extract in a separate bowl for approximately 3 minutes until fluffy.
3. Stir in the beaten egg until incorporated, then gradually add the dry ingredients to the bowl, mixing well until a dough forms.
4. Gather the dough and wrap loosely in a sheet of greaseproof paper, then leave to stand at room temperature for 2 hours.
5. Preheat the oven to 190°C (170°C fan) / 375F / gas 5 and line two baking trays with greaseproof paper.
6. Dust a work surface with flour and roll out the dough to 5 mm (¼ in) thickness.
7. Use a rectangular cookie cutter to stamp out playing card-sized pieces of dough, arranging them on the trays, spaced apart.
8. Stud the four corners of each piece with a blanched almond and shape the cherries into hearts with a small paring knife.
9. Press the cherry hearts into the centre of the cookies and bake for 12–14 minutes until golden and set.
10. Remove from the oven and leave to cool on the trays for 5 minutes.
11. Move to a wire rack to finish cooling before serving.

# Vanilla and Cardamom Cookies

**Makes** 24 **Preparation time** 55–60 minutes **Cooking time** 15–20 minutes

## Ingredients

1 vanilla pod, split lengthways with seeds scraped out

225 g / 8 oz / 1 cup caster (superfine) sugar

175 g / 6 oz / ¾ cup unsalted butter, softened

1 tsp vanilla extract

300 g / 10 ½ oz / 2 cups plain (all-purpose) flour, sifted

a pinch of salt

1 tsp ground cardamom

110 g / 4 oz / ½ cup granulated sugar

## Method

1. Combine the vanilla seeds and sugar in a food processor, pulsing until incorporated.
2. Tip into a bowl and cream with the butter and vanilla extract for 3–4 minutes until pale and fluffy.
3. Add the flour , salt and cardamom to the bowl, stirring well until a dough comes together.
4. Turn out the dough and knead gently, then roll into a cylinder, wrap in greaseproof paper and chill for 30 minutes.
5. Preheat the oven to 170°C (150°C fan) / 325F / gas 3 and line two baking trays with greaseproof paper.
6. Dust a work surface with the granulated sugar and roll the cylinder of dough into it, coating the outside evenly.
7. Cut the dough into discs and arrange on the baking trays, spaced apart.
8. Bake for 15–20 minutes until golden at the edges and set.
9. Remove from the oven and leave to cool on the trays for 10 minutes.
10. Move to a wire rack to finish cooling before serving.

# Ginger Snap Cookies

**Makes** 24 **Preparation time** 20 minutes **Cooking time** 18–22 minutes

## Ingredients

300 g / 10 ½ oz / 2 cups plain (all-purpose) flour, sifted

2 tsp bicarbonate of (baking) soda

a pinch of salt

1 tsp ground cinnamon

2 tsp ground ginger

175 g / 6 oz / ¾ cup unsalted butter, softened

225 g / 8 oz / 1 cup caster (superfine) sugar

1 large egg, lightly beaten

75 g / 3 oz / ¼ cup treacle

65 g / 2 oz / ½ cup icing (confectioners') sugar, sifted

a little boiling water

edible star sugar decorations (optional)

## Method

1. Preheat the oven to 180°C (160°C fan) / 350F / gas 4 and grease and line two baking trays with greaseproof paper.
2. Combine the flour, bicarbonate of soda, salt and ground spices in a large mixing bowl, stirring well.
3. Cream together the butter and sugar in a separate mixing bowl for 3–4 minutes until pale and fluffy, then add the egg and beat until incorporated.
4. Add the dry ingredients in two additions, mixing in the treacle between the additions.
5. Take scoops of the mixture and arrange on the baking trays, well spaced apart, flattening them out a little into rounds.
6. Bake for 18–22 minutes until golden, set and crisp at the edges, then remove to a wire rack to cool.
7. Mix the icing sugar with a little boiling water to make a smooth icing.
8. Decorate some of the cookies with the icing and star decorations, if desired.

# Chai with Cinnamon Stars

**Makes** 4 **Preparation time** 35–40 minutes **Cooking time** 10–12 minutes

## Ingredients

**For the cookies:**

110 g / 4 oz / ½ cup caster (superfine) sugar
60 g / 2 oz / ¼ cup unsalted butter, softened
1 small egg, lightly beaten
½ tsp vanilla extract
125 g / 4 ½ oz / ¾ cup plain (all-purpose) flour, sifted
a little extra plain flour, for dusting
½ tsp baking powder
1 ½ tsp ground cinnamon, plus extra for garnishing
a pinch of salt
55 g / 2 oz / ⅓ cup wholewheat flour
125 g / 4 ½ oz / 1 cup icing (confectioners') sugar, sifted
a little boiling water

**For the chai:**

4 cardamom pods
6 cloves
1 cinnamon stick, plus extra for garnishing
5 cm (2 in) piece of root ginger, peeled and sliced
500 ml / 16 fl. oz / 2 cups water
65 g / 2 oz / ¼ cup caster (superfine) sugar
6 Assam or Darjeeling tea bags
500 ml / 18 fl. oz / 2 cups whole milk

## Method

1. For the cookies: preheat the oven to 180°C (160°C fan) / 350F / gas 4 and line a large baking tray with greaseproof paper.
2. Cream together the sugar and butter in a large mixing bowl for 3–4 minutes until pale and fluffy.
3. Add the egg and vanilla extract, beating well for a further minute, then add the plain flour, baking powder, cinnamon and salt and mix well. Finally, add the wholewheat flour, stirring until a dough comes together.
4. Turn out the dough and knead briefly and gently into a ball. Roll out the dough on a lightly floured surface to 1 cm (½ in) thickness.
5. Using a star-shaped cutter, stamp out stars of dough and arrange on the baking tray, spaced apart. Bake for 10–12 minutes until golden and set.
6. Remove from the oven and leave the biscuits to cool on the trays for 10 minutes.
7. Mix the icing sugar with enough boiling water to make a spreadable icing.
8. Once the cookies have cooled enough, spread their tops with icing and leave to set on a wire rack.
9. For the chai: crush the whole spices and ginger with a mortar and pestle, then combine with the water and the sugar in a saucepan.
10. Heat over a moderate heat until simmering point, cooking steadily for 5 minutes. Remove from the heat and add the tea bags, stirring once, then leave them to steep for 5 minutes.
11. Discard the tea bags, add the milk and cook over a moderate heat until it approaches boiling point, stirring occasionally.
12. Strain the chai into serving glasses and garnish with a pinch of cinnamon and cinnamon sticks, serving with the biscuits.

# Novelty

# Iced Christmas Trees

**Makes** 18 **Preparation time** 1 hour 25–35 minutes **Cooking time** 18–20 minutes

## Ingredients

225 g / 8 oz / 1 cup unsalted butter, softened

175 g / 6 oz / ¾ cup caster (superfine) sugar

1 large egg, lightly beaten

1 tsp vanilla extract

300 g / 10 ½ oz / 2 cups plain (all-purpose) flour, sifted

a little extra plain flour, for dusting

2 tbsp cornflour (cornstarch)

a pinch of salt

a little icing (confectioners') sugar, for dusting

300 g / 10 ½ oz / 1 ½ cups white fondant icing

100 g / 3 ½ oz / ½ cup clear piping gel

white icing pen

silver dragee balls, to decorate

## Method

1. Cream together the butter and caster sugar in a large mixing bowl until pale and fluffy.
2. Add the egg and vanilla and beat well to incorporate, then add the flour, cornflour and salt.
3. Mix well until a dough comes together. Wrap the dough in cling film and chill for 1 hour.
4. Preheat the oven to 180°C (160°C fan) / 350F / gas 4 and line two large baking trays with greaseproof paper.
5. On a lightly floured surface, roll out the dough to 5 mm (¼ in) thickness.
6. Using a Christmas tree cookie cutter, cut out trees from the dough and arrange on the baking trays, well spaced apart.
7. Bake for 18–20 minutes until golden and set, then remove them from the oven.
8. Leave to cool on the trays for a few minutes, then move to wire racks to finish cooling.
9. Once cool, dust a work surface with a little icing sugar and roll out the icing to 5 mm thickness.
10. Using a smaller Christmas tree-shaped cutter or a sharp knife, cut out tree shapes from the icing.
11. Brush the top of the cookies with a little piping gel, then attach the icing trees to them.
12. Decorate with a white icing pen and silver dragee balls before serving.

# Iced Snowmen

**Makes** 18 **Preparation time** 1 hour 30–40 minutes **Cooking time** 15–18 minutes

## Ingredients

225 g / 8 oz / 1 cup unsalted butter, softened
175 g / 6 oz / ¾ cup caster (superfine) sugar
1 large egg, lightly beaten
1 tsp vanilla extract
300 g / 10 ½ oz / 2 cups plain (all-purpose) flour, sifted
a little extra plain flour, for dusting
2 tbsp cornflour (cornstarch)
a pinch of salt
100 g / 3 ½ oz / ½ cup clear piping gel
a little icing (confectioners') sugar, for dusting
300 g / 10 ½ oz / 1 ½ cups light blue fondant icing
white icing pen
a few drops of natural orange food dye
a few drops of natural red food dye

## Method

1. Beat together the butter and caster sugar in a large mixing bowl until pale and fluffy.
2. Add the egg and vanilla and beat well to incorporate, then add the flour, cornflour and salt.
3. Mix well until a dough comes together. Wrap the dough in cling film and chill for 1 hour.
4. Preheat the oven to 180°C (160°C fan) / 350F / gas 4 and line two large baking trays with greaseproof paper.
5. On a lightly floured surface, roll out the dough to 5 mm (¼ in) thickness.
6. Using a snowman cookie cutter, cut out snowmen from the dough and arrange on the baking trays, spaced well apart.
7. Bake for 15–18 minutes until golden and set, then remove from the oven.
8. Leave them to cool on their trays for a few minutes before moving to wire racks to finish cooling.
9. Once cool, dust a work surface with a little icing sugar and roll out the icing to 5 mm (¼ in) thickness.
10. Using a sharp knife, carefully cut out snowmen shapes from the icing.
11. Brush the top of the cookies with a little piping gel, then attach the icing to them.
12. Decorate with a white icing pen and then squeeze a little of the icing out into a small dish.
13. Paint the noses with the orange food dye and then place on the snowmen.
14. Use the tip of a sharp knife to score eyes and a smile on the faces, then dab the cheeks with a little red food dye.

# Gingerbread Decorations

**Makes** 24 **Preparation time** 2 hours 35–45 minutes **Cooking time** 10–12 minutes

## Ingredients

300 g / 10 ½ oz / 2 cups plain (all-purpose) flour, sifted
a little extra plain flour, for dusting
1 tsp baking powder
½ tsp bicarbonate of (baking) soda
a pinch of salt
2 tsp ground ginger
a pinch of ground cloves
110 g / 4 oz / ½ cup unsalted butter, softened
110 g / 4 oz / ⅔ cup soft dark brown sugar
65 g / 2 ½ oz / ¼ cup golden syrup
1 tsp vanilla extract
1 small egg, lightly beaten
375 g / 13 oz / 3 cups icing (confectioners') sugar, sifted
a little boiling water
a few drops each of pink, blue and purple natural food dye
assorted dragee balls
white icing pen

## Method

1. Combine the flour, baking powder, bicarbonate of soda, salt, ginger and cloves in a large mixing bowl, stirring thoroughly.
2. Beat together the butter, brown sugar, golden syrup and vanilla extract in a separate bowl until thick. Stir in the beaten egg until incorporated.
3. Gradually add the dry ingredients to the bowl, mixing well until a dough comes together, then wrap the dough loosely in a sheet of greaseproof paper and leave to stand at room temperature for 2 hours.
4. Preheat the oven to 190°C (170°C fan) / 375F / gas 5 and line two baking trays with greaseproof paper.
5. Dust a work surface with flour and roll out the dough on it to 5 mm (¼ in) thickness.
6. Use various shapes of cookie cutter to stamp out shapes of dough, arranging them on the trays, spaced apart.
7. Bore a small hole in each piece of dough towards the edge, then bake for 10–12 minutes until golden and set.
8. Remove from the oven and leave to rest on the trays for 5 minutes, moving to a wire rack to finish cooling.
9. Once cool, whisk the icing sugar with enough boiling water to make a smooth, spreadable icing.
10. Divide the icing between three bowls and decorate each with a separate food dye.
11. Spread the gingerbread with the icing and decorate with dragee balls and a white icing pen. then leave them to set.
12. Once set, thread with decorative ribbon or thread before hanging.

# Jam Star Cookies

**Makes** 12 **Preparation time** 1 hour 20–25 minutes **Cooking time** 12–16 minutes

## Ingredients

300 g / 10 ½ oz / 2 cups plain (all-purpose) flour

a little extra plain flour, for dusting

55 g / 2 oz / ⅓ cup cornflour (cornstarch)

a pinch of salt

65 g / 2 ½ oz / ½ cup icing (confectioners') sugar, plus extra for dusting

225 g / 8 oz / 1 cup unsalted butter, cubed

300 g / 10 ½ oz / 1 ⅓ cups strawberry jam (jelly), warmed

## Method

1. Pulse together the flour, cornflour, salt, icing sugar and butter in a food processor until they come together to form a dough.
2. Remove the dough, knead gently and form into a ball, then wrap in cling film and chill for 1 hour.
3. Preheat the oven to 180°C (160°C fan) / 350F / gas 4 and line two large baking trays with greaseproof paper.
4. Remove the dough from the fridge and roll out on a lightly floured surface to 5 mm (¼ in) thickness.
5. Cut out 24 shapes from the dough using a star-shaped cookie cutter.
6. Arrange on the baking trays, spaced apart, then use a small star-shaped cutter to punch stars out of half of them, arranging them next to the larger stars.
7. Bake for 12–16 minutes until they start to brown at the edges, then remove to a wire rack to cool.
8. Once cool, spread the complete star cookies with the warmed jam and sandwich against the remaining star cookies with the holes.
9. Dust with a little icing sugar before serving.

# Iced Star Cinnamon Cookies

**Makes** 24 **Preparation time** 25–30 minutes **Cooking time** 10–12 minutes

## Ingredients

225 g / 8 oz / 1 cup caster (superfine) sugar
125 g / 4 ½ oz / ½ cup unsalted butter, softened
1 large egg, lightly beaten
1 tsp vanilla extract
110 g / 4 oz / ⅔ cup plain (all-purpose) flour
a little extra plain flour, for dusting
1 tsp baking powder
1 ½ tsp ground cinnamon
a pinch of salt
110 g / 4 oz / ⅔ cup wholewheat flour
200 g / 7 oz / 1 ½ cups icing (confectioners') sugar, sifted
a little boiling water

## Method

1. Preheat the oven to 180°C (160°C fan) / 350F / gas 4 and line a large baking tray with greaseproof paper.
2. Cream together the sugar and butter in a large mixing bowl for 3–4 minutes until pale and fluffy.
3. Add the egg and vanilla extract and beat well for a further minute, then add the plain flour, baking powder, cinnamon and salt and mix well.
4. Add the wholewheat flour, stirring until a dough comes together, then turn out the dough and knead briefly and gently into a ball.
5. Roll out the dough on a lightly floured surface to 1 cm (½ in) thickness.
6. Using a star-shaped cutter, stamp out stars of dough and arrange on the baking tray, spaced apart.
7. Bake for 10–12 minutes until golden and set, then remove the biscuits from the oven and leave to cool on the trays for 10 minutes.
8. Mix the icing sugar with enough boiling water to make a spreadable icing.
9. Once the cookies have cooled enough, spread their tops with icing and leave to set on a wire rack before serving.

# Christmas Letter Cookies

**Makes** 24 **Preparation time** 1 hour 25–30 minutes **Cooking time** 15–18 minutes

## Ingredients

225 g / 8 oz / 1 cup unsalted butter, softened
175 g / 6 oz / ¾ cup caster (superfine) sugar
1 large egg, lightly beaten
1 tsp vanilla extract
300 g / 10 ½ oz / 2 cups plain (all-purpose) flour, sifted
a little extra plain flour, for dusting
2 tbsp cornflour (cornstarch)
a pinch of salt
100 g / 3 ½ oz / ½ cup clear piping gel
75 g / 3 oz / ⅓ cup white sugar crystals
75 g / 3 oz / ⅓ cup red sugar crystals

## Method

1. Beat together the butter and caster sugar in a large mixing bowl until pale and fluffy.
2. Add the egg and vanilla and beat well to incorporate, then add the flour, cornflour and salt.
3. Mix well until a dough comes together. then wrap the dough in cling film and chill for 1 hour.
4. Preheat the oven to 180°C (160°C fan) / 350F / gas 4 and line two large baking trays with greaseproof paper.
5. On a lightly floured surface, roll out the dough to 5 mm (¼ in) thickness.
6. Using letter-shaped cutters, stamp out letters from the dough and arrange on the baking trays, well spaced apart.
7. Bore small halls in the corners of the biscuits.
8. Bake for 15–18 minutes until golden and set, then remove from the oven.
9. Leave them to cool on their trays for a few minutes, then move to wire racks to finish cooling.
10. Once cool, brush with clear piping gel and decorate with the sugar crystals.
11. Thread the biscuits with string to hang, if desired.

# Gingerbread Men

**Makes** 16 **Preparation time** 1 hour 25–30 minutes **Cooking time** 10–12 minutes

## Ingredients

300 g / 10 ½ oz / 2 cups plain (all-purpose) flour, sifted

a little extra plain flour, for dusting

1 tsp baking powder

½ tsp bicarbonate of (baking) soda

a pinch of salt

2 tsp ground ginger

110 g / 4 oz / ½ cup unsalted butter, softened

110 g / 4 oz / ⅔ cup soft dark brown sugar

75 g / 3 oz / ¼ cup treacle

1 tsp vanilla extract

1 small egg, lightly beaten

225 g / 8 oz / 1 cup white fondant icing

a little boiling water

## Method

1. Combine the flour, baking powder, bicarbonate of soda, salt and ginger in a large mixing bowl, stirring thoroughly.
2. Beat together the butter, brown sugar, treacle and vanilla extract in a separate bowl until thick.
3. Stir in the beaten egg until incorporated and gradually mix in the dry ingredients until a dough comes together.
4. Gather the dough and wrap loosely in a sheet of greaseproof paper, then leave to stand at room temperature for 1 hour.
5. Preheat the oven to 190°C (170°C fan) / 375F / gas 5 and line two baking trays with greaseproof paper.
6. Dust a work surface with flour and roll out the dough on it to 5 mm (¼ in) thickness.
7. Use a gingerbread man cutter to stamp out the dough figures, arranging them on the trays, spaced apart.
8. Bake for 10–12 minutes until golden and set, then remove from the oven.
9. Leave the cookies to cool on their trays for 10 minutes and then move to a wire rack to finish cooling.
10. Once cool, prepare the icing by kneading it until soft.
11. Place in a bowl, mixing with enough boiling water until smooth and of pouring consistency.
12. Pour into a piping bag fitted with a small, round nozzle.
13. Pipe faces and various decorations onto the cookies, letting them set before serving.

# Stained Glass Hearts

**Makes** 24 **Preparation time** 1 hour 5–10 minutes **Cooking time** 15–18 minutes

## Ingredients

150 g / 5 oz / 1 cup strawberry boiled sweets

150 g / 5 oz / 1 cup apple boiled sweets

175 g / 6 oz / ¾ cup unsalted butter, softened

225 g / 8 oz / 1 cup caster (superfine) sugar

1 tsp vanilla extract

300 g / 10 ½ oz / 2 cups plain (all-purpose) flour, sifted

a pinch of salt

white icing pen

assorted dragee balls

## Method

1. Grind the boiled sweets separately in a food processor until they have the consistency of granulated sugar.
2. Cream together the butter, caster sugar and vanilla extract for 3–4 minutes until pale and fluffy.
3. Add the flour and salt to the bowl, stirring well until a dough comes together.
4. Turn out the dough and knead gently, then pat into a round, wrap in greaseproof paper and chill for 30 minutes.
5. Preheat the oven to 170°C (150°C fan) / 325F / gas 3 and line two baking trays with greaseproof paper.
6. Roll out the dough on a lightly floured surface to 1 cm (½ in) thickness.
7. Using a heart-shaped cutter, cut out hearts of dough and then use a smaller heart-shaped cutter to cut out heart-shaped holes from their centres.
8. Arrange the hearts on the baking trays, spaced apart and fill the holes with the ground sweets, levelling them flat with a small palette knife.
9. Bore a small hole at the top of the dough, then bake for 15–18 minutes until the cookies are golden at the edges and the fillings have melted.
10. Remove from the oven and leave them to cool on the trays for 10 minutes.
11. Move to a wire rack to finish cooling.
12. Once cool, decorate with an icing pen at the borders and the dragee balls on top.
13. Thread the holes with decorative ribbon or thread before hanging.

# Mulled Wine with Gingerbread

**Serves** 4 **Preparation time** 1 hour 20 minutes **Cooking time** 10–12 minutes

## Ingredients

**For the cookies:**

300 g / 10 ½ oz / 2 cups plain (all-purpose) flour, sifted

a little extra plain flour, for dusting

1 tsp baking powder

½ tsp bicarbonate of (baking) soda

a pinch of salt

2 tsp ground ginger

110 g / 4 oz / ½ cup unsalted butter, softened

110 g / 4 oz / ⅔ cup soft dark brown sugar

75 g / 3 oz / ¼ cup treacle

1 tsp vanilla extract

1 small egg, lightly beaten

110 g / 4 oz / 1 cup cashews

**For the mulled wine:**

1 tsp cloves

4 star anise

5 cm (2 in) piece of cinnamon stick

100 g / 3 ½ oz / ½ cup caster (superfine) sugar

1.25 l / 2 pints 4 fl. oz / 5 cups light-bodied red wine

## Method

1. For the cookies: combine the flour, baking powder, bicarbonate of soda, salt and ginger in a large mixing bowl, stirring thoroughly.
2. Beat together the butter, brown sugar, treacle and vanilla extract in a separate bowl until thick.
3. Stir in the beaten egg until incorporated and gradually mix in the dry ingredients until a dough comes together.
4. Gather the dough and wrap loosely in a sheet of greaseproof paper., then leave to stand at room temperature for 1 hour.
5. Preheat the oven to 190°C (170°C fan) / 375F / gas 5 and line two baking trays with greaseproof paper.
6. Dust a work surface with flour and roll out the dough on it to 5 mm (¼ in) thickness.
7. Use the gingerbread man cutter to stamp out the dough figures, arranging them on the trays, spaced apart.
8. Gather any remaining dough and re-roll, then cut out small rounds and stud with cashew nuts.
9. Arrange around the gingerbread men and then bake for 10–12 minutes until golden and set.
10. Remove from the oven and cool on a wire rack.
11. For the mulled wine: heat a large saucepan over a moderate heat until hot, add the spices and dry-fry for 30 seconds. Add the caster sugar and half of the wine, stirring well.
12. Heat until simmering, stirring from time to time, until the sugar has dissolved. Add the remaining wine and return to a steady simmer for 45 minutes.
13. Pour into glasses and serve with the gingerbread men.

# Free From

# Dairy-free Spiced Cookies

**Makes** 18 **Preparation time** 20–25 minutes **Cooking time** 20–25 minutes

## Ingredients

400 g / 14 oz / 2 cups canned chickpeas (garbanzo beans), drained

110 g / 4 oz / ½ cup smooth peanut butter

½ tsp ground cinnamon

½ tsp ground nutmeg

a pinch of ground cloves

½ tsp vanilla extract

½ tsp baking powder

¼ tsp bicarbonate of (baking) soda

a pinch of salt

75 g / 3 oz / ⅓ cup maple syrup

1 large banana, mashed

100 g / 3 ½ oz / ⅔ cup raisins, roughly chopped

## Method

1. Preheat the oven to 180°C (160°C fan) / 350F / gas 4 and line a large baking tray with greaseproof paper.
2. Combine all the ingredients apart from the raisins in a food processor and process for approximately 2 minutes until well combined.
3. Add the raisins and pulse a few times until incorporated.
4. Drop small balls of the dough onto the lined baking tray, spaced apart and flatten slightly with a fork.
5. Bake for 20–25 minutes until golden and set.
6. Remove from the oven and leave to cool on the tray for 10 minutes before moving to a wire rack.
7. Serve once warm or when completely cooled.

# Gluten-free Rum Bites

**Makes** 24 **Preparation time** 2 hours 20 minutes **Cooking time** 5–10 minutes

## Ingredients

350 g / 12 oz / 2 ⅓ cups white chocolate, chopped

250 ml / 9 fl. oz / 1 cup double (heavy) cream

75 ml / 3 fl. oz / ⅓ cup coconut rum liqueur

125 g / 4 ½ oz / 1 cup icing (confectioners') sugar

## Method

1. Place the chocolate in a heatproof bowl and set to one side.
2. Heat together the cream and liqueur in a saucepan set over a medium heat until almost boiling.
3. Pour over the chocolate, leaving it untouched for one minute.
4. After a minute, stir until smooth, then cover the bowl with cling film.
5. Chill for 2 hours until firm but not set.
6. Take scoops of the mixture between your palms and roll into truffles.
7. Arrange on a lined tray and dust the rum bites in icing sugar before serving.

# Gluten-free Almond Cookies

**Makes** 24 **Preparation time** 1 hour 20–25 minutes **Cooking time** 15–18 minutes

## Ingredients

110 g / 4 oz / ½ cup unsalted butter, softened
175 g / 6 oz / ¾ cup caster (superfine) sugar
a little extra caster sugar, for dusting
1 large egg, lightly beaten
1 tsp almond extract
150 g / 5 oz / 1 cup gluten-free plain (all-purpose) flour, plus extra for dusting
2 tbsp cornflour (cornstarch)
100 g / 3 ½ oz / 1 cup ground almonds
a pinch of salt
½ lemon, zested
75 g / 3 oz / ¾ cup almonds, split in half

## Method

1. Cream together the butter and sugar in a mixing bowl for 3–4 minutes until pale and fluffy.
2. Stir in the egg and almond extract, then add the flour, cornflour, ground almonds, salt and lemon zest.
3. Combine until a dough comes together. Turn out onto a floured surface and knead briefly and gently, gathering it into a ball.
4. Divide the dough in half, roll each half into cylinders and wrap in greaseproof paper.
5. Chill for 1 hour until firm.
6. Preheat the oven to 180°C (160°C fan) / 350F / gas 4 and line two large baking trays with greaseproof paper.
7. Remove the dough from the fridge and cut into discs, arranging them on the trays, spaced apart.
8. Stud half of the discs with halved almonds, then bake the biscuits for 15–18 minutes until golden and set.
9. Remove from the oven and dust immediately with a little caster sugar, leaving the biscuits to cool on their trays for 10 minutes.
10. Move to a wire rack to finish cooling before serving.

# Gluten-free Apricot Cookies

**Makes** 24 **Preparation time** 15–20 minutes **Cooking time** 15–18 minutes

## Ingredients

150 g / 5 oz / 1 cup gluten-free plain (all-purpose) flour, sifted

100 g / 3 ½ oz / 1 cup ground almonds

a pinch of salt

½ tsp gluten-free baking powder

175 g / 6 oz / ¾ cup unsalted butter, softened

150 g / 5 oz / ⅔ cup caster (superfine) sugar

1 large egg, lightly beaten

½ tsp vanilla extract

150 g / 5 oz / 1 cup cocktail cherries in syrup, drained and chopped

110 g / 4 oz / ½ cup apricot jam (jelly), warmed

100 g / 3 ½ oz / ¾ cup flaked (slivered) almonds

## Method

1. Preheat the oven to 180°C (160°C fan) / 350F / gas 4 and grease and line a large baking tray with greaseproof paper.
2. Combine the flour, ground almonds, salt and baking powder in a large mixing bowl and stir thoroughly.
3. Beat together the butter and sugar in a separate mixing bowl for 3–4 minutes until pale and fluffy.
4. Add the egg and vanilla extract, beating well to incorporate.
5. Add the dry ingredients in two additions, beating until a cookie dough comes together, then stir the cherries into the dough.
6. Take small scoops of the dough and arrange on the baking tray, spaced apart.
7. Flatten slightly with your thumb before topping with a brush of warmed apricot jam and a sprinkle of flaked almonds.
8. Bake for 15–18 minutes until golden and set.
9. Remove to a wire rack to cool before serving.

# Dairy-free Pistachio Macaroons

**Makes** 32 **Preparation time** 30–35 minutes **Cooking time** 12–14 minutes

## Ingredients

250 g / 9 oz / 2 cups icing (confectioners') sugar, sifted

a little extra icing (confectioners') sugar, for dusting

110 g / 4 oz / 1 cup ground almonds

75 g / 3 oz / 1 cup desiccated coconut

2 large egg whites

a pinch of salt

½ tsp almond extract

75 g / 3 oz / ¾ cup shelled pistachios, finely chopped

## Method

1. Preheat the oven to 180°C (160°C fan) / 350F / gas 4 and grease and line two large baking trays with greaseproof paper.
2. Combine 250 g / 9 oz / 2 cups of icing sugar with the ground almonds and desiccated coconut in a large mixing bowl.
3. Beat the egg whites with a pinch of salt in a separate mixing bowl until stiffly peaked.
4. Fold the egg whites and almond extract into the ground almond mixture until combined, then add the pistachios and fold them into the mixture gently until well mixed.
5. Scrape the mixture into a piping bag fitted with a large, round nozzle.
6. Pipe 32 rounds onto the baking trays, spaced apart, and dust with the remaining icing sugar.
7. Leave them to set for 15 minutes, then bake for 12–14 minutes until set and starting to brown and crack.
8. Remove to a wire rack to cool before serving.

# Gluten-free Thumbprint Cookies

**Makes** 24 **Preparation time** 20 minutes **Cooking time** 15–18 minutes

## Ingredients

150 g / 5 oz / 1 cup gluten-free plain (all-purpose) flour, sifted

100 g / 3 ½ oz / 1 cup ground almonds

a pinch of salt

½ tsp gluten-free baking powder

175 g / 6 oz / ¾ cup unsalted butter, softened

150 g / 5 oz / ⅔ cup caster (superfine) sugar

1 large egg, lightly beaten

½ tsp vanilla extract

55 g / 2 oz / ⅓ cup dried cranberries, finely chopped

75 g / 3 oz / ⅓ cup cranberry jam (jelly)

55 g / 2 oz / ½ cup flaked (slivered) almonds, roughly chopped

## Method

1. Preheat the oven to 180°C (160°C fan) / 350F / gas 4 and grease and line a large baking tray with greaseproof paper.
2. Combine the flour, ground almonds, salt and baking powder in a large mixing bowl and stir thoroughly.
3. Beat together the butter and sugar in a separate mixing bowl for 3–4 minutes until pale and fluffy.
4. Add the egg and vanilla extract, beating well to incorporate.
5. Add the dry ingredients in two additions, beating until a cookie dough comes together, then stir in the chopped dried cranberries.
6. Take small scoops of the dough and arrange on the baking tray, spaced apart.
7. Flatten slightly with your thumb before making a small indent in half of the rounds of dough.
8. Fill the indent with a little jam and stud the edges of the cookies with flaked almonds, spacing them apart.
9. Bake for 15–18 minutes until golden and set, then remove to a wire rack to cool before serving.

# Dairy-free Bites with Spiced Apple Juice

**Makes** 24 **Preparation time** 20–25 minutes **Cooking time** 12–14 minutes

## Ingredients

**For the bites:**

85 g / 3 ½ oz / ⅔ cup icing (confectioners') sugar

75 g / 3 oz / 1/3 cup apricot jam (jelly)

225 g / 8 oz / 1 cup dairy-free margarine, softened

1 tsp vanilla extract

300 g / 10 ½ oz / 2 cups gluten-free plain (all-purpose) flour, sifted

2 tbsp gluten-free cocoa powder

½ tsp salt

75 g / 3 oz / ½ cups dried apricots, chopped

150 g / 5 oz / 1 cup cocoa nibs

225 g / 8 oz / 1 cup demerara sugar

**For the spiced apple juice:**

1.25 l / 2 pints 4 fl. oz / 5 cups apple juice

5 cm (2 in) cinnamon stick

1 tsp cloves

1 orange, sliced

## Method

1. For the cookies: preheat the oven to 200°C (180°C fan) / 400F / gas 6 and line a large baking tray with greaseproof paper.
2. Cream together the icing sugar, apricot jam and margarine in a mixing bowl for 3–4 minutes until pale and fluffy.
3. Add the vanilla and beat for a further minute until incorporated.
4. Combine the flour, cocoa powder and salt in a separate bowl, then add to the creamed margarine mixture in two additions, mixing thoroughly.
5. Add the chopped apricots and cocoa nibs, mixing well to incorporate.
6. Take heaped tablespoons of the dough and shape into balls between your palms, then roll the balls in demerara sugar and arrange on the baking tray, spaced apart.
7. Bake for 12–14 minutes until they just begin to crack.
8. Remove to a wire rack to cool as you prepare the cider.
9. For the spiced apple juice: combine the apple juice, spices and orange in a saucepan set over a medium heat. Warm until simmering.
10. Simmer gently for a further 10 minutes, stirring occasionally. Keep warm over a low heat and ladle into glasses, serving with the bites on the side.

# INDEX